The Cross-Examination Edge

A Guide to Effective Questioning

Peter D. Polchinski

Lawyers & Judges Publishing Company, Inc.
Tucson, Arizona

P.O. Box 30040 • Tucson, AZ 85751-0040
(800) 209-7109 • FAX (800) 330-8795
e-mail: sales@lawyersandjudges.com
www.lawyersandjudges.com

ISBN 13: 978-1-933264-27-1
ISBN 10: 1-933264-27-6
Printed in the United States of America
10 9 8 7 6 5 4 3 2 1

For Jean and Casey

Contents

Introduction

A. My answer is: I hope I never run into you again!
—An orthopedic surgeon, ready to leave the witness stand

Cross-examination has been called "the greatest legal engine ever invented for the discovery of truth" (John Henry Wigmore). Cross-examination ("cross") is your chance to confront and challenge the other side's testimony. The witness has told his story during the direct examination ("direct"), and now must remain in the witness box and answer your questions.

This is a how-to book. The focus is on how to cross-examine during a jury trial, but it will also show the reader how to confront any witness, in any kind of trial, hearing or proceeding, formal or informal. Some of the techniques can also be used in lively conversation, but you should be gentle with friends and family.

At trial, witnesses have one natural advantage over the lawyer: The jury knows that the witness is at the lawyer's mercy; he must patiently answer the lawyer's questions without objection, and he cannot ask his own questions. Jurors therefore empathize with them, and tend to give them the benefit of the doubt. Witnesses can hold their advantage by being humble and honest, but they often get themselves into trouble on the stand by becoming advocates. They volunteer information beyond the scope of the question; they give opinions and conclusions that are self-serving; they try to match wits with the questioning lawyer; they stretch the truth and they lie. When they do so, they lose their favored status, for two reasons. First, nobody likes a smart aleck. Second, the jury knows that the questioning lawyer is just doing her job, but the witness is not doing his job, which is to answer questions simply and honestly. When the witness starts to misbehave, even slightly, he levels the playing field, and the advantage shifts to the lawyer.

The lawyer can gain more leverage and credibility by consistently showing fairness and by being even-tempered. There is a time and place for righteous indignation, anger and sharp words, but they should be used sparingly. Cross-examination does not mean that you must be cross. You should get the job done, but also be pleasant and likeable. When the jury likes you, they will be more likely to trust you.

Finally, the lawyer must overcome the natural fear that accompanies any daring endeavor, and turn it into exhilaration. Cross-examination allows a lawyer to take command of the courtroom, to reveal the truth to everyone present, and often to either win the case or secure a favorable resolution for the client. Except for the occasional pro-se litigant, only lawyers have the privilege of questioning a witness in open court. It is a unique opportunity to do something important and challenging.

Fear is natural, but it can be conquered with experience. As a practical matter, during cross, you are in total control; nothing happens until you speak. The witness is not allowed to ask questions, and when his answers are sarcastic, long-winded or nonresponsive, you can show the jury through your questions and demeanor that he is acting inappropriately. Bear in mind also that you know your case, both the facts and the law, better than the witness; and with adequate preparation, a positive attitude, and the skills you will acquire from this book, you can and will prevail on cross.

Therefore, when the judge turns and says: "Cross-examination, Counselor," rise from your chair and walk briskly to the lectern. Approach the witness as you would any adversary—with respect and caution, but without fear.

Author's Note: I have included samples of cross-examinations throughout this handbook. Many are from my own trials, several are from cases I have seen or read about over the years, a few are from movies, and others are fictional. The sample questions cover a variety of common courtroom scenarios, and the new lawyer can use them as a starting point for cross preparation. The seasoned advocate should find a few lines to add to the trial notebook. In practice, when you create your own questions, preserve them for easy reference, to avoid having to re-invent the wheel for each case.

—Peter D. Polchinski (February 2010)

I

Preparation for the Witness

Counsel: Let me re-phrase it. It was kind of poorly phrased.
The Court: Most of your questions are, but that's okay. Want to start over?

Preparation is the key to success in court. Every witness examination requires understanding, imagination, and knowledge of the facts and that is especially true of cross. The office time invested in reviewing the file is time well spent.

Prepare for each adverse witness before trial. Review all transcripts, statements, reports, or any other documents the witness prepared. Circle or highlight all of the important facts in those documents and have them ready for use at trial. When the file includes a report prepared by someone who evaluated the witness during discovery, study the report and note the witness's strengths and weaknesses. Have a purpose and a plan for every witness.

Sit back and think.

Before trial and after a day in court, spend time alone. Sit behind a closed door, at a clean desk, with your feet up, and think about your case. Write down thoughts and observations on a legal pad, and preserve them. The palest ink is better than the most retentive memory" (Confucius).

Consider the nine non-collateral areas.

Even when there are no pre-trial statements or testimony, you can and must prepare for cross in advance. To do this, review the nine areas of inquiry that are not collateral; that is, they are so fundamental to the discovery of truth that the law allows questioning on cross even when they are not mentioned on direct examination.

The nine areas are:

1. Oath (does truth matter?).

Example: The witness is a postmodern anarchist who believes truth is whatever she thinks that day. If she will not promise to tell the truth (as truth is commonly understood), then she should not be permitted to testify.

2. Ability to perceive (could the witness see or hear?).

Example: The witness has poor eyesight or hearing, or was not in a position to observe the incident.

3. Ability to recall (how is his memory?).

Example: A witness may remember that it took 12 seconds to get from point A to point B, but he cannot even approximate how long he has been on the witness stand.

4. Ability to communicate (can the witness tell us?).

Example: A witness may not be able to speak, write, or otherwise communicate in a comprehensible manner.

5. Bias (favors one side).

Example: The witness has been a fan of the celebrity defendant for more than 20 years.

6. Prejudice (is against one side).

Example: The witness is a business rival with a history of conflict with the plaintiff.

7. Interest (stands to gain or lose by the outcome).

Example: A spouse will most likely benefit from the other spouse's recovery of money damages.

8. Bad acts (is the witness bad enough to be untrustworthy?).

Example: The witness set fire to the neighbor's gazebo.

9. Criminal convictions (obtain a certified copy).

Review the nine areas when you prepare questions for cross, especially for a non-party or surprise witness, or the other side's family member or close friend.

Evaluate the witness.

Consider each adverse witness before trial, and ask: What will she say, and how will it hurt the case? Can the witness help? Determine whether the witness is truthful, mistaken, exaggerating or lying. You will be tougher with the apparently sympathetic person who is a liar, than with the honest but mistaken ex-convict.

Your initial evaluation may change during the direct—the witness originally thought to be lying may, in fact, be mistaken. Adjust your questions and demeanor accordingly.

Use your common sense and life experience. Try to determine whether the other side's conduct and prior testimony about it was reasonable and logical, and ask: Is this how people behave in the real world? Of course, apply those same tests to your own client and witnesses, as well.

Organize the examination.

Adverse witnesses often have information that will help the case. As a general rule, try the following order for cross:

First, obtain favorable testimony, or friendly concessions, early in the cross, while the witness is still confident. Begin the examination in a calm and cordial manner—a talkative witness will provide helpful testimony.

Second, have the adverse witness corroborate your position. Introduce undisputed facts that support your side. When your witnesses have already testified, have their witnesses corroborate your witnesses.

Third, have the witness contradict or discredit the other side's witnesses. Challenge him with another adverse witness's different testimony about an important fact.

Finally, attack the testimony or the witness or both.

If, however, there is powerful evidence to discredit the witness, then deliver it with the first question:

Q. Are you the same Attila who sacked all of those cities?
A. The same.

Write the questions.

Write or type your cross questions before trial, and use separate pages for each topic. Leave several spaces between each question so that additional questions can be inserted. The text should be large and legible. Write your two or three most important questions again at the end of your notes, to avoid omitting them.

Use simple Mother Goose language (Judge Kevin T. Duffy) and remember that the spoken word differs from the written word. Write the questions as they will be delivered, but be careful when using contractions; did and didn't are easily confused by the listener.

At trial, do not read the questions—keep the notes on the lectern and refer to them only when necessary. Cross requires more flexibility than direct—the witness's answers will require you to improvise and change course more often.

Listen to the direct.

Listen carefully to the direct. Do not write down the entire examination—watch the witness and occasionally glance at the jury. Write only what you will use for cross, or might use for summation, and use a separate page for each topic.

Use two legal pads: One for the prepared cross, and one for the direct testimony. Keep a red pen at counsel table, and write a bold red Q next to an answer on direct by the witness that you will challenge on cross. Write helpful answers word for word. Bring both pads to the lectern, for easy reference.

II

Questioning Techniques

The question is were you lying then or are you lying now or in fact are you a chronic and habitual LIAR!

–Sir Wilfrid (*Witness for the Prosecution*)

Deliver statements of fact.

On cross, leading questions are not only permitted, they are essential for success. They should not merely be leading, they should be brutally leading. The most effective questions are statements of fact: instead of asking a question, the lawyer provides the answer as a fact, and directs the witness to acknowledge it as true. Observe three different ways of asking the same question, non-leading, leading and statement of fact:

Q. Where were you on December 12?
A. In Reno (non-leading).

Q. Were you in Reno on December 12?
A. Yes (leading).

Q. You were in Reno on December 12.
A. Yes (statement of fact).

Most questions on cross should be short statements of fact that the witness must admit or deny. A fact statement ends with a period (or exclamation point), and not a question mark:

Q. You never resigned.
A. Not really, no.
Q. You were fired.
A. Yes, I was.
Q. And told to leave.
A. Right.
Q. And to not return.
A. Yeah.

Statements of fact are more effective and persuasive than questions, because the witness has less room to wriggle out or tailor her answers. When a fact is stated boldly and without hesitation, the jurors will believe the fact is true, and the witness is more likely to admit that it is true:

Q. Did you have three drinks?
A. Maybe two, I'm not sure.
Q. Sir, you had three drinks.
A. Yes… alright, I did.

Make sure that the statements sound like questions, and not testimony, in order to avoid objections. Practice before trial, and adjust the inflection of your voice accordingly.

Inquire in good faith.

Assert only those facts that you either know or honestly believe are true. When the evidence shows that the witness consumed one drink, do not accuse her of having three. But when the witness admitted before trial that she had three drinks or other evidence supports it, then confront her with that fact. Do not be concerned about causing discomfort to the witness. When the facts sought are true, relevant and important to the case, the jury must hear them.

Expand statements into repetitive strings.

Repetitive strings are groups of questions (statements) that expand an area of cross by dividing a line of inquiry into a series of facts, each covered by one question. The string of questions highlights each fact, leads to a series of yes or no answers and allows you to control the witness:

Q. Mr. Van Weasel, you are the President, Chairman of the Board and Chief Executive Officer of the company?
A. Yes.

Becomes:

Q. Sir, you are the company President.
A. Yes.
Q. You are the Chairman of the Board.
A. Yes.
Q. And also the Chief Executive Officer.
A. I admit I am all three.

Note how the technique expands the last verse of Jimmy Buffett's *Margaritaville* from one question into eight questions:

Q. Sir, isn't it a fact that you blew out your flip flop, stepped on a pop top, cut your heel and had to cruise on back home?
A. Yes.

Becomes:

Q. You blew out your flip flop.
A. Yes.
Q. Stepped on a pop top.
A. Yes.
Q. Cut your heel.
A. Right.
Q. And had to cruise on back home.
A. I did.
Q. But there was booze in the blender.
A. There was.
Q. And soon it did render.
A. What?

Q. That frozen concoction.
A. Yes.
Q. That helps you hang on.
A. True.
Counsel: That's it. Thank you.

Practice the technique until it becomes second nature. State a series of facts with repetitive strings that the witness must confirm or deny. Avoid compound questions—provide one fact at a time. When you are tempted to ask one or two questions, subdivide the area of inquiry further and ask a string of ten or more questions. Do not be concerned about sounding tiresome or redundant. Develop a rhythm and forge forward, and the jury will follow every question and answer.

Lay a foundation for admissions and concessions.

Effective cross includes introducing favorable admissions and obtaining concessions that support your position at trial. An admission is a pre-trial statement by the other side. According to Professor Irving Younger, it is anything the other side said that has something to do with the case. A concession is an acknowledgement that the admitted conduct was significant and important.

To obtain admissions and concessions on cross, you must lay a foundation with questions that lead the witness to the ultimate answer you seek. A foundation includes basic, non-confrontational questions such as the person's training, duties and experience. The witness will readily answer the foundation questions, and she will set the stage for the damaging testimony.

Obtain the concession before the admission.

When you have an admission that you plan to introduce, have the witness concede that the conduct was significant before you introduce the admission. The theory behind this approach is that a witness will be more cooperative before he is attacked or embarrassed.

For example, assume that a company requires security guards to check all locked doors on every round, and in his incident report, the guard admitted he did not check the doors on his 7:00 p.m. round.

Also, assume that failure is a key fact in the case. His statement that he did not check the doors is an admission. An acknowledgement that checking the doors was important would be a concession. The admission alone will help the case, but adding the concession would double the impact.

Because the witness admitted before trial that he did not check the doors, he will probably admit that on the stand. If he doesn't, you will impeach him, using the techniques shown in Chapter 3. The goal here would be to obtain a concession; to have him admit that his oversight was important. The foundation required to secure the concession is to establish the importance of the conduct before the witness admits what he did. That is, obtain the concession before introducing the admission.

The jury must hear the concession first, because when the witness admits his conduct before he is asked about its significance, he will probably deny that it was important. To avoid the denial, use the improved version, instead of the initial version, both shown after the introductory questions:

Q. You have been with the company for 12 years.
A. Right.
Q. You received training when you started.
A. Yes.
Q. And it's fair to say you're experienced on the job.
A. I would agree.
Q. On the day in question, you came on duty at Noon.
A. Yes.
Q. You worked a full shift.
A. I did.
Q. You checked the doors at 4:00 p.m.?
A. Yes.
Q. They were locked.
A. They were.

Initial version:

> Q. You made rounds again at 7:00 p.m.
> A. Yes.
> Q. You did not check the doors at seven.
> A. No, not then.
> Q. It's important that you check them.
> A. Only, if necessary.
> Q. Isn't it required at every round?
> A. Not really—I do have discretion.

Improved version:

> Q. It's important to check them.
> A. Yes.
> Q. At every round.
> A. Generally, yes.
> Q. It's required that you do that.
> A. It is.
> Q. But you did not check them at seven.
> A. No, I didn't.

In the initial version, the witness had to admit his conduct first, and he was stung by his admission. Afterward, he refused to concede that he should have checked the doors. Instead, he defended his conduct by re-interpreting company policy.

In the improved version, the witness had already conceded that it was important to check the doors (the foundation), and when he stated that he had not checked them, it was too late to deny the significance of his actions. Always lay the foundation and get the concession before the admission.

III

Impeachment with Prior Inconsistent Statements

Sympathy is a wonderful human emotion, but it has no place in fact finding.

– Judge Gerald S. Held

Impeachment (challenging or discrediting) with prior inconsistent statements is the art of confronting a witness with a statement or testimony, given before trial, which is materially different from the witness's testimony at trial. For example, when a witness testifies at trial that the traffic light was red for your driver, but in a pre-trial statement to an investigator, the witness said that your driver had a light turning amber, then the witness should be impeached with the pre-trial statement. The purpose is to challenge the witness's credibility, or discredit the in-court testimony, or both. An effective impeachment can neutralize or even destroy a witness's testimony. To impeach correctly and successfully, you must show the inconsistency before the witness can explain it.

Find the admissions and be ready to impeach.

Adverse witnesses often provide admissions favorable to your case in pre-trial testimony, signed statements and reports. As the trial date approaches, they review those pre-trial statements, and often regret what they have said, because their original statements will damage their position at trial.

On the stand, a witness will often try to improve the statement she provided before trial. Basic facts such as time, speed, distance, ability to perceive, professional experience, and the witness's conduct before, during and after the event suddenly become more favorable to her case. Memories also improve remarkably. Whereas, at a deposition the witness has no idea how something occurred, at trial she provides the answer in lucid detail.

For example, a witness may have told an investigator or police officer that her speed was 35 miles per hour. Later, she learned the speed limit was 30 miles per hour. That witness will have a strong incentive to reduce her speed to 30, to avoid an allegation that she was speeding.

To prepare for impeachment, review all pretrial testimony and statements, one sentence at a time. Note the facts that are helpful to your side, and those facts the witness did not know, or did not remember. Anticipate which answers the witness will try to change and be prepared to impeach with those answers.

If, for example, the witness stated before trial that the red truck was traveling 45 to 50 miles per hour, and that speed helps your case, then be ready to confront the witness with his statement. For quick reference at trial, write the witness's pre-trial answers to important questions in your cross outline:

Speed of red truck—(45 to 50, Deposition page 33, line 7).

Use the R.A.C. technique.

The R.A.C. (pronounced "Rack") technique is a method of showing the jury that the witness's pre-trial testimony is closer to the truth than her in-court testimony.

R.A.C. is: Re-commit, Accredit and Confront. On cross, Re-commit the witness to his present, in-court testimony on direct, Accredit the pre-trial testimony or statement, by showing that it was carefully considered, honest and accurate, and Confront the witness with that earlier evidence, by framing the question so that the jury hears the evidence before the witness can explain it away. The R.A.C. technique can be used to impeach with any kind of inconsistent pre-trial evidence.

Impeach with deposition testimony.

When the witness's trial testimony about a material fact differs from his deposition testimony, impeach him with the R.A.C. technique. First, use repetitive strings and re-commit the witness to his in-court testimony. Note that the italicized words qualify the direct testimony as the present testimony, and not the truth:

Q. On direct, you testified about the speed of the red truck.
A. Yes.
Q. You told us, *on direct*, that the red truck was travelling 30 to 35 miles per hour.
A. Yes, that's right.
Q. You had thought about the speed before coming to court.
A. Yes.
Q. *And today*, you're sure that the truck was travelling 30 to 35 miles per hour.
A. That's correct.

Next, after having re-committed the witness to his in-court testimony, accredit the deposition testimony; that is, have the witness admit that the testimony was also given under oath and was therefore as important as the trial testimony.

After handing the judge a copy of the deposition transcript, use repetitive strings to establish that the deposition testimony was true and accurate. Do not ask the witness if he recalls or remembers either the deposition or a particular answer. The witness testified, and the transcript in your hand is proof that he testified, even if he has not read it. The truth is being revealed, and if the witness has no recollection, then that's his problem:

Q. You testified at a deposition for this case.
A. I believe so.
Q. About one year ago.
A. Yes.
Q. You took an oath at the deposition.
A. Yes.

Q. The same oath that you took today.
A. Yes, I was sworn.
Q. You were asked questions.
A. I remember that.
Q. And you gave answers to those questions.
A. I did.
Q. Your answers were truthful.
A. Yes, they were.
Q. And they were accurate.
A. Yes.
Q. You read the transcript afterward.
A. I did read it.
Q. You made sure that your answers were correct.
A. Yes.
Q. Then you signed the transcript.
A. I signed it.

Finally, confront the witness with the deposition testimony. The impeachment question, shown below, must be precise when you confront with prior testimony. Do not ask: "Didn't you say in your deposition," or, "You said something different before," or use any other variation. Preserve the following words on a legal pad or index card:

Q. Reading from your deposition of (January 10, 2010) at page (33) line (7), "Question (How fast was the red truck going)? Answer (45 to 50 miles per hour)"—Were you asked that question and did you give that answer?
A. Yes.

The witness has been impeached: He was attacked with his own words before he could explain why his testimony changed. Stop there and pause for a few seconds, to let the jury understand the importance of the changed testimony.

After the witness has been impeached, do not argue with him about the inconsistency. When you do, he will try to reconcile the two different answers and spoil the moment:

Q. Those two statements are different, right?
A. Not really, no. The speed of the red truck changed. He slowed down before the impact.

Also, avoid the often used, but argumentative and annoying: "Is your memory better now than it was at the time of your deposition?" Or: "Remember Sir, you are under oath."

Do not show the witness the transcript to refresh his recollection. We refresh *our* witnesses, and impeach *their* witnesses. When you show the transcript before impeaching him, he will try to explain the inconsistency. Deny him that opportunity. He will probably try to explain the difference during re-direct examination, but it will be too late!

Overcome the stubborn witness.

When the witness does not answer, or denies that she gave that answer, or wants to look at the transcript, read the confronting question again. Should the witness not admit that she testified as it was read, then turn to your adversary and say: "Counsel, did I read that question and answer correctly?" That is one of the few times you address opposing counsel directly before the jury.

Since the court now has a copy of the transcript, should your adversary refuse to respond (which is rare, but it happens), ask the judge the same question: "Your Honor, did I read the question and answer correctly?" The judge will most likely acknowledge that you read it correctly. If the judge appears impatient or annoyed, do not be intimidated: Make sure that the jury hears the inconsistency.

After receiving confirmation from counsel or the court that the transcript was read accurately, the witness may nevertheless insist that she does not remember that answer, as if to suggest that she never gave it. Should that occur, admonish the witness, but don't argue with her:

A. (Volunteered) I don't know if I said that.
Q. Well, if you said that, did you mean to say it?
A. I don't know what I said.

Q. You do not deny that it is in the transcript.
A. No.
Q. And you cannot deny that those are your words.
A. I can't deny it, no.
Q. Let's move on. . .

Try, as an alternative, Max D. Steuer's stinging reply:

Q. Don't you realize that your statement that you have no recollection does not deny that you said it?

Find the errata sheet.

Always check the correction or errata sheet at the end of every deposition transcript, to make sure that the witness has not changed the answer used for impeachment. Sometimes a witness will change an answer in a manner that is so obvious of a fabrication that it is comical. When the witness has done so, impeach him with his correction:

Q. Reading from page 14, line 10, Question, (What caused you to fall on the steps), Answer, (I have no idea), Correction from the errata sheet, two months later: (I fell because of a chipped, cracked, depressed, trap-like dangerous nuisance of long-standing on the step), Were you asked that question and did you give that answer and later correct it as read?
A. I guess so.

Be alert for creative corrections, but when a correction appears to be sincere and logical, do not impeach with that question and answer.

Discredit with a signed statement.

Impeach with the same R.A.C. method. After you re-commit the witness to her in-court testimony, accredit the earlier statement, and confront her with her statement.

Q. You spoke to an investigator some time after the accident?
A. I did speak to somebody about the accident.

Q. He came to your house.
A. Yes.
Q. You told him about the accident.
A. Yes.
Q. What you saw that day.
A. Yes.
Q. You were honest.
A. Of course.
Q. And accurate.
A. Sure.
Q. It was closer in time to the accident than today.
A. It was.
Q. As you told him the facts, he wrote them down.
A. He did.
Q. Then you read what he had written.
A. Yes.
Q. He had written what you had told him.
A. Yes.
Q. It was accurate.
A. Yes.
Q. And true.
A. Yes.
Q. After you made sure that it was accurate, you signed the statement.
A. Yes, I did.
Q. You told him the red truck was driving 45 to 50 miles per hour.
A. Yes, I probably did, if it's in there.

When the witness wants to see the statement, circle her signature with your pen, show the witness the document, and ask if that is her signature. When she wants to read the document, insist that she answer your questions first. Be bold—the truth is on your side. After you have impeached the witness, if she still wants to see the document, then circle the inconsistent statement and tell her to read only the part that you circled.

Challenge with a report.

When the witness prepares a report and he deviates from his report at trial, impeach him. Also, often a witness will include facts A, B, and C in his report, and at trial will add fact D to his testimony. Impeach the witness who adds important facts that are not in his report, and remember to lay the foundation before the impeachment:

Q. Detective Tracy, you told us on direct that Fred Goodman had stolen property with him that night.
A. That's right.
Q. No doubt in your mind.
A. No sir.
Q. And that is an important fact in this investigation.
A. Sure it is.
Q. Sir, it is part of your job to prepare a report.
A. Yes.
Q. And that is done when the event is fresh in your mind.
A. Yes.
Q. You prepared a report in this case.
A. I did.
Q. On the day of the arrest.
A. Yes.
Q. The facts were fresh in your mind.
A. They were.
Q. Your report was truthful.
A. Sure.
Q. It was accurate.
A. Yes.
Q. It included all of the important facts.
A. I suppose.
Q. Well, did it?
A. Yes.
Q. And you already told us that if one of the defendants had stolen property on him, then that is an important fact.
A. Yes, that would be important.
Q. Yet you never put in your report that Mr. Goodman possessed stolen property.
A. (Looking at report) No, I guess not.

Or:

Q. Please show us where in your report it says that Mr. Goodman had possessed stolen property.
A. (Looking at report) It's not there.
Q. You never put anything about stolen property in your report.
A. No.

Raise the issue when the witness avoids it.

To avoid possible impeachment at trial, sometimes opposing counsel will try to ignore the prior admission entirely (in our red truck case for example, they would not ask any questions about the speed of the truck). When that happens, use the witness's pre-trial statement or testimony to create contradictions during your cross.

Present the fact to the witness with his own words. Do not begin your question with, "You said in your deposition," or "Didn't you say in your statement," because the witness will detect trouble and will provide an excuse for the earlier statement. Just state the fact. When the witness admits the fact, it is an admission. When he denies or changes the fact, impeach him. Be sure to ask the question correctly:

Instead of:

Q. You said in your deposition that the red truck was traveling 45 to 50 miles an hour.
A. That must be a mistake. It was 30 to 35.

Try:

Q. The red truck was traveling 45 to 50 miles per hour, true?
A. Yes. (Admission).
A. No, 30 to 35. (Impeach him).

Create contradictions with non-leading questions.

Witnesses often testify before trial that they have no knowledge or recollection of significant facts. At trial, re-visit those "I don't know" and "I don't recall" answers with non-leading questions, by compiling a list of them and asking the same questions asked at the deposition or hearing. When the witness suddenly recovers his memory, impeach him with the prior "I don't know/recall" answer:

Q. Where did you go with the car after you left your house?
A. I don't recall.
Q. How many of you were in the car?
A. I don't know.
Q. Well, who was sitting where, in the car?
A. I don't remember.
Q. Anybody have a shotgun in the car?
A. There was no shotgun in the car. (Answer at hearing: I don't know.)
Q. Oh, really? (Impeach him.)

An added benefit of the above technique is that even if it does not lead to an impeachment, the witness loses some credibility by failing to have answers to many important questions.

Apply the escalation technique.

Lead the witness into an inconsistency by escalating to his prior statement. For example, when the witness testified before trial that the moon was brilliant that night, try the following questions, delivered by Patrick L. McCloskey:

Q. The moon was out that night.
A. Yes, it was.
Q. It was a full moon?
A. Yes.
Q. The moon was fairly bright.
A. Sure.
Q. In fact, the moon was brilliant that night.

A. I wouldn't say brilliant, no.
Q. You wouldn't? (Impeach him.)

Reject the creative explanation.

A clever adversary will have the witness, on direct, attempt to reconcile a prior inconsistent statement with the in-court testimony. The witness may also blurt out an explanation during your cross. When either occurs, do not abandon the point—impeach the witness so that the jury hears the inconsistency. Then, during your summation, tell the jury that the attempt by opposing counsel and the witness failed, because the two statements are inconsistent and cannot be reconciled.

For example, in one case, a wheelchair-bound plaintiff claimed that a bus driver caused his wheelchair to tip over backward, by using the bus's wheelchair lift improperly. The bus driver had stated, however, that the plaintiff leaned back in the wheelchair and tipped over by himself, and the wheelchair lift was not the cause of the accident. At his deposition, the plaintiff testified that a moment before he fell over, he was looking up at the sky, which was consistent with the bus driver's statement. At trial, the plaintiff attempted to tailor his trial testimony to explain his deposition testimony, in order to establish that he was not leaning back in his chair. He thus testified that he was "looking straight ahead, you know, up at the sky." The plaintiff was impeached with his deposition testimony, and in summation, the jury was told that the statements are inconsistent:

> Counsel (during summation): You remember how the plaintiff tried to harmonize his deposition testimony, which was the truth, with his trial testimony, which was false…straight ahead is a completely different direction than up at the sky, and the two statements cannot be said to mean the same thing…

Choose your battles wisely.

Decide which points to contest before trial. An attack on minor differences reduces the impact of the major contradictions. Avoid confronting a witness over a small or inconsequential difference. In other words, don't nitpick:

Q. In your statement you said the briefcase was maroon, in your deposition you said burgundy, and today in court you say cranberry. Which is it?
A. I thought they were all the same color.

Make sure the impeachment helps the case. Do not impeach if the earlier statement is even more damaging than the trial testimony:

Q. So, you admit that my client was only driving 65 miles per hour on Colorado Boulevard, and not 80, as you said in your statement to the investigator.
A. Right. But you know 80 might be more accurate. The little old lady sure was driving fast.

Remember your objective.

Keep your eye on your goal, which is to expose testimony that is less-than-honest. Be tough when necessary—it's part of the job. In the red truck example, the witness deliberately tried to help the case by reducing the speed of the truck at trial. Make the aggressive witness pay for her advocacy. Be careful, however, with one who is honestly mistaken. (See the "Avoid Fighting Words" section in Chapter 4).

Re-visit the inconsistency on re-cross.

On re-direct, your adversary will attempt to rehabilitate the witness. The witness will explain and reconcile her inconsistent statements. On re-cross, remind the jury of the impeachment:

Q. You told us about the speed of the red truck.
A. Yes.
Q. In court today it was 30 to 35 miles per hour, but at your deposition it was 45 to 50.
A. Yes, but I said why the speeds are different.
Q. But those speeds are different.
A. Yes, they are.
Counsel: Thank you. That's all, your Honor.

IV

Cross Techniques

If you haven't struck oil in 10 minutes, stop boring.

–Monsignor John McGuire

Start strong.

Introduce yourself and tell the witness your client's name. Explain that you will be asking questions about the case. Instead of: "If you do not understand my question, please tell me," try: "If I don't make myself clear, please tell me and I will ask another question." The latter form sounds less condescending, and when a witness does not understand a question, it is probably your fault. Do let the witness know by your tone and presence that you will be controlling the examination.

Because you will be seeking short acknowledgements to your statement questions, try: "If you can answer with a yes or no, please do so." That informs both the witness and the jury that you expect to hear yes or no answers.

Finally, do not begin your cross with: "I want to clarify a few things." The jury knows that your purpose is not to clarify the direct, but rather, to neutralize or discredit it.

Stand close to the jury.

When conducting cross, stand at the end of the jury box, near jurors 6 and 12. Some lawyers think it is clever to stand on the other side of the courtroom during cross, so that the witness is forced to look at the lawyer, and not at the jury. Later, in summation, that same lawyer will argue that the witness refused to look the jury in the eye. It is a courtroom tactic that is easily exposed: When your adversary conducts his cross from across the room, tell the jury in summation that the tactic was a cheap carnival trick designed to show that the witness was not trustworthy, when it was actually the lawyer who was trying to pull the wool over your eyes! Show the jury that you treat everyone fairly, and that you want each witness to look at the jury. Stand at the end of the jury rail for every witness.

Re-state only the favorable direct testimony.

Do not have the witness repeat the direct examination in the hope that it will sound better the second time. It will not. And unless the witness has flipped, that is, abandoned the other side and joined your side, he will not change his testimony when asked the same questions that opposing counsel asked. The witness will bolster the direct if permitted.

Use the direct testimony when it is helpful, but when its truth is doubtful, avoid re-stating the testimony as if it were true. Qualify the testimony with the words shown below, and refer to it as a mere claim.

Instead of:

Q. Mr. More, my client, cheated you out of money?
A. Yes.
Q. He left you destitute?
A. Yes.

Try:

Q. It's your testimony that Mr. More cheated you out of money.
A. Yes.
Q. You've told this jury that he left you destitute.
A. I am destitute!
Q. That's your silver Bentley parked in front of the courthouse?
A. Yes, but it's a rental.

Know the answer to your question.

Unless you are prepared to deal with the answer, or the answer does not matter, know the answer before asking the question, to avoid an unpleasant surprise:

Q. Mr. Defendant, I see that you walk with a limp. How did that come about?
A. Oh, that's nothing—just an old war wound. I was lucky I got a Bronze Star for it, in addition to the Purple Heart.

Reserve the "why" question.

The witness will be eager to explain some of her answers. Let her do so on re-direct. Only ask "why" when the answer does not matter, when you can impeach with an admission, when you have cut off every avenue of escape, or when there is no reasonable, innocent explanation:

Q. Well, while you were watching Mr. Baker's store, your competition, burn to the ground, tell the jury why you never called the fire department.
A. I really cannot recall.

James Blackburn provides an excellent example of how to ask "why" questions, when the witness's version is unreasonable and not credible. Mr. Blackburn was the prosecutor in the trial of Captain Jeffrey MacDonald, an army surgeon who was charged with the murders of his wife Colette and two young daughters, Kimberly and Kristen, at their home at Fort Bragg. Dr. MacDonald claimed that crazed hippies entered his house and brutally killed his family. However, he was present when the attacks occurred, and he suffered minor injuries that were not life-threatening. An unusual fact in the case was that each of the MacDonald family members had a different blood type, and that was crucial to the investigation. There was also evidence that someone at the murder scene had worn surgical gloves.

Mr. Blackburn used a variation of the "why" question, by contrasting the superb forensic evidence with the defendant's dubious claims, in a masterful cross. The testimony is recounted in the book *Fatal Vision*, by author Joe McGinniss, but here are a few samples:

> Q. Suppose the jury finds from the evidence that in that bedspread there is a seam thread matching your blue pajama top entwined around a hair with blood on its shaft matching that of your wife Collette—do you have any explanation for that?
> A. No.
> Q. Suppose the jury should find from the evidence that pieces of rubber or latex are found in that bundle of bedding on the floor. Do you have any explanation for that?
> A. I have none.
> Q. Suppose the jury should find from the evidence that the word PIG on the headboard over the bed where your wife slept was written in Type A blood with a gloved hand. Do you have any explanation for that?
> A. I have no explanation for that.

> Q. Suppose the jury should find, Doctor MacDonald, that Type AB blood, the same as that of your daughter Kimberly, was found on the blue pajama top; and that you were not wearing that pajama top when you went to see Kimberly. Do you have, sir, any explanation for that?
> A. Pure conjecture.
> Q. Is that your answer?
> A. Pure conjecture that any of us can make.
> Q. Well is that—do I take it then that any answer that you give would just be, as you said, conjecture on your part?
> A. It's pure conjecture, again.

> Q. Doctor MacDonald, did you take the bedspread and that sheet from the master bedroom off the floor, place Colette on the bedspread, step in blood on that bedspread, and pick Colette up and carry her out of the room?

A. I did not.
Q. Should the jury find from the evidence that the blood on the Old Hickory knife was wiped off on that bathmat, and also that the ice pick found outside the house was wiped off on it, do you, sir, have any explanation for that?
A. Not unless the assailants did that.
Q. Doctor MacDonald, suppose the jury should find from the evidence that the blood in the bathroom sink is Type B, your blood. Do you have any explanation for that?
A. No.

Confront with exact words.

While listening to the direct, write important answers word for word. Cross the witness with his exact words. When he denies that he used those words, ask the judge to have that portion of the direct re-read to the jury. If it cannot be read at that time, speak to the court reporter later, obtain a copy of that transcript page, and read it in your summation.

Counsel (during summation): Remember when the defendant denied that he said the pedestrian was sort of stupid and should have been more careful. Reading his direct testimony from page 207 of our Trial Transcript, line 18: The pedestrian was sort of stupid and should have been more careful.

Do not demand a "yes or no" answer.

Lawyers often end their questions on cross with: "Yes or no," and sometimes do so throughout the cross. That technique should be used rarely, because the lawyer sounds like a bully. Instead, phrase your questions so that "yes," "no," "I don't know" or "I do not remember" are the only logical answers. When the witness persists in avoiding a simple question, try:

Q. Can't you answer that with a Yes or No?
A. I'm not sure.
Q. Well, would you please try to?

Avoid fighting words.

People who are honest but mistaken become indignant when you attack their competence as witnesses. To obtain admissions and concessions from an honest witness, do not be harsh. Use words that appeal to their sense of honesty and fairness. Do not accuse the witness with fighting words such as (you were) careless, foolish, inattentive, hostile, furious, lazy, ignorant or disgruntled.

Note the cross of a waitress who testified that your client started the fight, and see how the fighting words, in the first example, insult and energize the witness:

Q. You saw the men at the table.
A. Yes.
Q. They were just talking then.
A. Yes.
Q. Then you turned and faced the bar.
A. Right.
Q. You spoke to the bartender.
A. Yes.
Q. You gave him your drink order.
A. I did.
Q. Then you looked back at the table.
A. Yes.

Fighting words:

Q. So, you were distracted and not really paying attention.
A. No, I was not distracted. I saw your client start the fight.

Improved version:

Q. Fair to say you took your eyes away from the table for just a few seconds?
A. Yes, I suppose I did.

Resist one question too many.

In the example above, the witness's answers on cross may undermine the direct and establish that she could not have witnessed what she claims to have witnessed. Do not ask a question that will allow her to salvage her testimony:

Q. So, you never really saw who started the fight that night.
A. No, I saw it plain as day. It was your client. That man sitting there (indicating).

In one case, defense counsel tried to suggest that his client's confession was obtained after the defendant asked for a lawyer, which would have been a clear violation of his Miranda right to remain silent. During his cross of the homicide detective, counsel asked one question too many:

Q. Detective Bowman, did my client at any time ask for a lawyer?
A. No.
Q. Did he ask for food?
A. I don't remember that.
Q. Well, did he ask for water?
A. Not that I can recall.
Q. If you don't remember anything about food or water, how can you be sure he never asked for a lawyer?
A. (Leaning forward) Because if he had asked for a lawyer, I would have stopped questioning him.

Establish facts, and not conclusions.

When you suggest conclusions, impressions or characterizations to the witness, you invite an argument:

Q. The bar room was really crowded?
A. I wouldn't say really crowded, no.

Instead, lay a foundation to obtain a logical conclusion with the probability cross:

Q. You were in the bar room?
A. Yes.
Q. It was 5:30 in the evening.
A. Yes, it was.
Q. On a Friday.
A. Yes.
Q. It was happy hour.
A. Yes.
Q. There were many customers at the bar.
A. Yes, a lot.
Q. You had to squeeze through, to get to the dining room.
A. Oh, yes.
Q. And the tables in the dining room were filled.
A. They were.
Q. Fair to say the place was crowded?
A. Yes, it was.

Let the witness complete her answer.

Rejoice when a witness rambles and does not respond to your question. Do not stop the witness in mid-sentence or mid-paragraph. Let her finish her answer. Her credibility is hurt when she does not answer your question honestly. The non-responsive answer also provides an opportunity for you to discipline the witness and exert greater control over the examination:

Q. Mr. Tipton, for the third time, are you sure it took 5 minutes to prepare those grits?
A. I may have been mistaken.

When the witness tries to evade the question, repeat the question with the same words, and be persistent. The jury will know the witness is being difficult, and not you:

Q. Sheriff Farley, did the defendant repeat your words when he said I shot the clerk?
A. He admitted to the homicide.
Q. But did he merely repeat your words when he said I shot the clerk?

A. He admitted that he shot the clerk.
Q. But Sir, did he repeat your words, I shot the clerk?
A. He might have.

When the witness still refuses to answer, try:

Q. Don't you want to answer that question?

Or:

Q. Sir, will you please answer the question I asked, and not the question you wish that I had asked.

Or:

Q. Please tell the jury why you will not answer that question for them.

Don't ask the judge for help.

Avoid: "Please, your Honor, tell the witness to answer my question." A plea for help places the judge in the uncomfortable position of co-counsel. When your questions are concise, the judge will probably assist you without a request. You should, however, occasionally rebuke an uncooperative witness by moving to strike non-responsive testimony:

Counsel: Your Honor, I move to strike the last answer as nonresponsive.
The Court: Strike it out. Mr. Bossy, please answer the question.

When your adversary responds that the answer was responsive, ask to have the question and answer re-read:

Counsel: Your Honor, I move to have the last answer stricken as nonresponsive.
Opposing Counsel: Judge, the answer was completely responsive.

Counsel: Your Honor, may we have the question and answer read back.
The Court: Yes, Madam Reporter, please read it back.
Reporter: "Question, Didn't you fire Ms. Jones one hour after she refused to go out with you? Answer, I fired her for cause, and I was completely justified."
The Court: Strike it out as non-responsive.

The above technique is effective because it exposes both the witness and opposing counsel as being less-than-honest.

Press for an answer.

When you need a vital admission or concession, be persistent and press the witness for the answer:

Q. Your company never removed the toxic waste, did it?
A. I am not sure what time period you are referring to.
Q. Sir, I said never. Your company never removed the waste.
A. Right. We never removed it.

Also, do not abandon an important point because opposing counsel objects or the judge is impatient. Stand firm and show counsel and the court that you will not be bullied:

Q. Mr. Del Vermo, I'd like an answer to my question.
The Court: He gave an answer.
Q. Your Honor, respectfully, he gave an answer to some other question, not mine.
The Court: Very well. (To the Reporter) Read it back.

Note: "Respectfully" is the proper term when you disagree with the judge. When a lawyer says "with all due respect," he means "you're an idiot" (Judge Ruth Moskowitz).

Limit the use of question headers and tag endings.

Headers are question introductions; tag endings are question add-ons. Trial lawyers commonly use both. Lawyers cannot resist starting questions with "isn't it a fact that" or "isn't it true that," or ending them with "isn't that correct," or "isn't that right," or "did you not?" Some lawyers even repeat the same ones incessantly.

Use headers and tag endings sparingly, and vary them, to avoid sounding redundant. Also, do not respond to answers with: "I see."

Re-phrase "isn't it possible."

When a question begins with "isn't it possible," your adversary may object by saying anything is possible, and the objection will probably be sustained. Actually, the contention that anything is possible is simply untrue. More things are impossible than are possible. For example, one cannot jog from New York to Paris, or make phone calls to Mars. Nevertheless, the objection anything is possible is usually sustained. To avoid the problem, use variations of "could have" and "you don't know whether":

Q. Isn't it possible that she entered by the window of the bathroom?
Opposing Counsel: Objection, anything is possible.
The Court: Sustained. Re-phrase it.
Q. She could have entered by that bathroom window?
A. Maybe.
Q. You don't know whether she came in through the bathroom window.
A. She might have.

Omit "do you know" and "do you recall."

Question headers "do you know" or "do you recall" allow the witness to answer no and avoid the question. Instead of providing that escape for him, phrase your questions so that he must say "I don't know" or "I don't recall." In other words, let the witness reveal his faulty memory to the jury:

Instead of:

Q. Do you recall whether Mr. Bailey's house was in Bedford Falls?
A. No, not really.

Try:

Q. Mr. Potter, wasn't Mr. Bailey's house in Bedford Falls?
A. I don't remember.

Build your case with an adverse witness.

Consider how a witness against your side can help. Accentuate positive facts and eliminate negative facts—have the witness tell the jury about favorable evidence the witness found and unfavorable evidence she did not find:

Q. Officer Molloy, when you arrested Mr. Friendly, he gave you no trouble.
A. No, he was cooperative.
Q. Never tried to run.
A. No.
Q. In fact, he was surprised that you confronted him.
A. He did look surprised, but that happens.
Q. And he asked you: "What's this all about?"
A. Right.
Q. Then you told him about the robbery.
A. I did.
Q. And he still had no idea what you were talking about.
A. That's what he said.
Q. He had a wallet in his pocket?
A. Yes, he did.
Q. He had valid identification.
A. What do you mean by valid?
Q. He had a driver's license.
A. Yes.
Q. He had an I.D. card from his job.
A. Yes.

Q. He also had family photos.
A. Yes.
Q. Of his wife and children.
A. Right.
Q. He had work gloves in his pocket.
A. He did.
Q. He had work boots on.
A. Yes.
Q. He had no stolen property with him.
A. No, he had none.
Q. None whatsoever.
A. Right.
Q. No weapon of any kind.
A. True.
Q. No gun?
A. No gun.
Q. No knife either?
A. Correct.
Q. Nothing to indicate that he had committed any robbery.
A. Right.
Q. Nothing that would suggest he had committed any crime at all.
A. That's true.

Deliver small summations on cross.

Where appropriate, preview your final argument through a repetitive string of questions:

Q. You told us that you use extra care when approaching that intersection.
A. That's right.
Q. Because you know that the intersection is in a residential area.
A. Yes.
Q. There are many people there.
A. True.
Q. Many children.
A. Yes.

Q. Especially in the early evening.
A. Yes.
Q. During the summer.
A. I agree.
Q. And it's important to use extra care when there are children near the roadway.
A. Yes, it is.
Q. Because a child might step into the roadway.
A. Right.
Q. As young Tommy Tucker did here.
A. Yes.

Admonish the witness who uses legal terms.

A witness, usually a party to the case, may use legal terms that he learned from his lawyer or someone else. Often that language is part of the applicable law for the case, and the witness wants to help prove the claim or defense by including it in the testimony. Confront him with the language used:

Q. Mr. Creed, I notice that you have repeatedly used the term "extraordinary and violent jerk," to describe the movement of the train, true?
A. Yes.
Q. That's a legal term, isn't it?
A. I think so.
Q. That is not a phrase that you use every day.
A. No.
Q. You learned that term from someone else.
A. Yes.
Q. Just for this lawsuit.
A. Right.
Q. Did you know that term is the standard required to prove your case?
A. (To the judge) I don't know how to answer that.
The Court: Counsel, I think you've made your point.

Address the family member.

When the other side calls a family member or close friend to testify, establish the family bond and be alert for canned responses:

Q. You are the defendant's sister.
A. Yes.
Q. You both live in the same house.
A. Yes.
Q. You both came to court together.
A. Yes.
Q. And you have come to court to help his case?
A. Yes, but I wouldn't lie for him.
Q. Who said anything about lying?
A. I don't understand.
Q. Did someone suggest that you say "I wouldn't lie for him" when you were questioned?
A. I don't remember.

Surprise the surprise witness.

Although in most courts witnesses are disclosed before trial to avoid trial by ambush, sometimes a surprise witness appears. If your objection to the witness is overruled, then have a short list of questions to show the jury that he is, in fact, a surprise, last minute addition to the case:

Q. Sir, have you testified before in this case?
A. In this case? No.
Q. Did you give a statement to anybody about this case?
A. No.
Q. When were you contacted about testifying?
A. Last night, by phone.
Q. Last night? Who called you?
A. The lawyer there.
Q. Had you ever spoken to him before?
A. No.
Q. How did he get your name and number?

A. I don't know.
Q. Were you surprised to get the call?
A. Actually, I was.
Q. Would it be fair to describe you as a surprised witness?
Opposing counsel: Objection. Did he say surprise witness or surprised witness?
The Court: I think he meant both.

Remember also to return to the nine non-collateral areas for anyone who is not a party, eyewitness, or expert.

Visit the scene.

Always visit the scene of the incident, and take notes and photographs while you are there. A ten-minute inspection can provide great insight. Determine whether the area has changed since the event in question. Confront the witness with details about the scene:

Q. Isn't the candy store across the street from the bakery?
A. Well, maybe.
Q. And not next door.
A. I'm not sure.
Q. The firehouse is next door.
A. You're right . . . I was wrong. I don't remember that block too well.

Observe and create.

Use the power of observation and your imagination. Watch the witnesses inside and outside the courtroom. When an independent, non-party witness is too friendly with the opposition, question him about it while he is on the witness stand. Ask him how many times he spoke to or met with opposing counsel, and what they talked about. Ask who paid his carfare, and how he traveled to court. When he has notes, ask to see them. Consider every bit of information available as potential ammunition for cross. Follow your instincts and take chances.

When the witness looks at opposing counsel after your questions, try F. Lee Bailey's question:

Q. Sir, I see you looking over at counsel there after I ask a question. Please tell us why you are doing that.

Reprimand a witness who laughs sarcastically or otherwise inappropriately during your cross:

Q. Mr. Jester, do you find this court proceeding to be funny?

Add drama to the presentation.

Be aware of what is occurring in the courtroom, and whenever possible, add drama to your presentation. Vary your pace, tone and demeanor. Pause after an important answer. When appropriate, show confusion, disbelief, understanding, annoyance or other emotions, without being melodramatic. Seize opportunities for excitement when they arise. Also, don't be a crank—have a light-hearted approach to the amusing incidents that invariably occur. And avoid frowning if the jury is laughing.

In one case, an aspiring actor testified before trial that his past employment included a position at Propaganda Films, a legitimate film production company with a sinister, or ironic, name. The witness provided his work history willingly at his deposition, but he became nervous about it before the jury. Note too that his lawyer, unlike the jury, did not appreciate the humor of the moment:

Q. You have worked at your present job for one year.
A. Yes.
Q. (Accusingly) Sir, before your present job, didn't you work for Propaganda Films?
A. (To the judge) Do I have to answer that?
Opposing Counsel: Objection!
The Court: Overruled. (To the witness) Yes, you have to answer.
A. Well, I didn't really work for them, it was more like free-lance.
Q. (Louder, and with more emphasis) Never mind free-lance. Isn't it a fact, Sir, that you worked for Propaganda Films!

Opposing counsel: Objection.
The Court: Overruled. Answer the question.
A. (Reluctantly) Yeah, I did work for them.

Show fairness and kindness.

Be aware of human sensibilities. Although you may have occasion to tease a witness as shown above, do not intentionally humiliate or embarrass a witness or anyone else in the courtroom. When you discredit a witness or otherwise cause anxiety, do not gloat. Also, show consideration when you inquire about a delicate matter:

Q. Mr. Tanaka, please forgive me for this question, but I must ask you how much you weigh.
A. No problem—four-fifty.

In the movie *My Cousin Vinny*, defense attorney Vincent LaGuardia Gambini combined creativity with a warm heart to win a point. He suggested that eyewitness Mrs. Riley's thick eyeglasses needed to be upgraded, but the witness disagreed. To test her vision, he walked to the back of the courtroom with fifty feet of tape measure, held up two fingers, and asked the witness to state how many fingers he was displaying. When Mrs. Riley said "Four," he returned to the well of the court while showing his two fingers, and stated:

Q. What do you think now, Dear?
A. I'm thinking of getting thicker glasses.

Win the small confrontations.

Make sure the jury knows when you have impeached a witness, or caught her in a contradiction or lie. Every point you contest on cross-examination is a small trial—there is a winner and a loser. Some lawyers contend that you should save it for summation, that is, proceed with subtlety, let the jury figure out what just happened, (if they can), and explain the point in summation. The better practice is to show the jury by your questions and tone that your version of the fact in issue makes more sense than the witness's version, and that you have won the point. Save your arguments for summation, but win the small battles on cross. During summation, revisit the point, explain to the jury why your version is more reasonable, and tell them why it is important.

Chip away at the direct.

Do not feel compelled to demolish the witness. Instead, try to chip away at the witness's story. During your career, there will be times when you will overwhelm the witness and discredit the entire direct testimony. Most often, that will not happen. Do the best with what you have. Identify areas where the witness is vulnerable and limit your questions to those areas. The cross will be successful when it casts doubt upon one part of the direct.

Pass the witness who does no harm.

You need not question every witness. When an adverse party has been called for a limited purpose, such as to authenticate records, or the testimony has not damaged your case, then stand after the direct and say: "No questions, your Honor." Then sit down.

Stop sooner, rather than later.

Consider the sage advice about cross from an old-time Brooklyn lawyer: Get in, make your points, and get out. There is no need to drone on and beat a dead horse. The jurors will remember a short, tight and effective examination.

End with a strong point.

Throughout your cross-examination, stand straight and speak directly and confidently. Be tough, but fair. Avoid sarcasm. Keep your composure, even after a harmful answer. Accept the blame when you phrase a question poorly, and start again. End with a strong point, and then return to counsel table. Sit down with your head held high, but without arrogance or malice.

V

Preparation for the Expert

Q. Doctor, would you be surprised if you saw the defendant talking to himself?
A. Not in the least.
Q. Why is that?
A. He doesn't have any friends.

Study the expert's report.

As you would with any lay witness, review carefully all documents prepared by the expert. Circle or highlight every finding and conclusion. Determine whether the facts that support the opinion are accurate. When the opinion is not supported by the evidence that will be produced at trial, you may have a ground for excluding the expert.

Compare any Notice of Expert provided by counsel with the expert's report. The contentions in the notice may differ from the conclusions in the expert's report.

Examine the curriculum vitae.

Determine whether the educational and professional background on the expert's resume is accurate. Some experts embellish, and others create pure fiction. Beware of unlisted honors and achievements that surface at trial. When the expert introduces a previously undisclosed honor on direct, lay the foundation and remind the jury of it on cross.

Investigate the expert's publications. The expert may claim to be the author of a book, when he is merely the co-author of a chapter.

In one case, a chiropractor's curriculum vitae included Graduate Studies at the end of his education credentials. The entry was vague, and it did not include the year or institution, and it was worthy of inquiry. The following exchange took place:

Q. Dr. Richards, your resume includes the term Graduate Studies.
A. Yes.
Q. What were they?
A. Well, that was a seminar I attended in Houston.
Q. How long was the seminar?
A. Two days.
Q. And that's what you would consider Graduate Studies?
A. Yes.
Q. What would you call a Masters or Ph.D. program at a university?
A. That would also be Graduate Studies.
Q. The same as your two-day seminar.
A. Right.

Compare transcripts of prior testimony.

Learn how the expert has answered basic questions in past trials by comparing her testimony in other cases. Include important answers in your notes, along with the case name, the court where the trial was held, and the judge's name. When the expert's opinion about the same ultimate issue was different in an earlier case with similar facts, lay a foundation and impeach her with her prior testimony.

Search the Internet.

Use the Internet to research both the expert and the subject. Determine whether the expert has a website, and if he does, then see how he promotes himself. Find articles he claims to have written, and compare his conclusions to his position in your case.

Read the records sent to the courthouse.

Have your investigator serve subpoenas for all of the pertinent documents for the case, such as medical and employment records. Review the records in the courthouse record room and prepare notes for use on cross. Bend or dog ear the top corners of the two or three most important pages, so that you can find them quickly.

Check jury verdict summaries.

Review published jury trial summaries to determine whether the adverse expert always testifies for one side: that is, prosecution or defense, or plaintiff or defendant. When she appears to be a partisan expert, but will not admit it, ask about the percentage of cases for each side:

Q. Doctor, when you come to court, isn't it almost always for the defense?
A. That's not true. I testify for both sides.
Q. Well, in the past years, in what percentage of cases did you testify for the defense?
A. Oh, maybe 95 percent.

Also, when she has testified as an expert in highway design in one case and as an expert in toaster ovens in another, she might be a jack-of-all-trades.

Compile a list of all of her areas of expertise, and on cross, expose her as a so-called expert on everything:

Q. Mrs. Hinds, you've testified as an expert on stairways.
A. Yes.
Q. That's why you're here today.
A. Correct.
Q. You have also been called as an expert on skateboards?
A. Yes.
Q. On microwave ovens.
A. Right.

Q. On electric blankets.
A. Yes, once.
Q. Also on golf carts.
A. I do recall that.
Q. And if I continue through the Jury Verdict Reporter, a total of 22 different products, appliances, tools and vehicles.
A. I'll take your word for it.
Q. Is there anything sold on the market today that you would hesitate to testify about?
A. Perhaps some kinds of sophisticated medical equipment.
Q. But not much else.
A. No.

Consult learned treatises.

When a treatise on the subject contradicts the adverse expert, bring the book to court. Have the expert admit that it is authoritative, and then confront him with the pertinent entries. The clever expert will refuse to accept any treatise as authoritative, and when you approach him with the book, he may even recoil as if you were holding a rattlesnake:

A. No, no, I won't look at that!
Q. (Approaching the witness) Take it easy, Doctor. It's only a textbook.

When the witness refuses to acknowledge a textbook as authoritative, try some of the following questions, and be prepared for the witness to fight every point:

Q. Doctor, you say this book is not authoritative, even though it's in its 3rd Edition?
A. That's right.
Q. Would you admit that it must have been authoritative to somebody, after all the years it has been in print?
A. I can't imagine who that might be.
Q. As an example of somebody, how about the faculty of the Harvard Medical School?

A. I would be surprised to learn that!

Q. Did you see that 3 of the contributors to the book are on the faculty of that medical school.

A. I did not see that, but it still does not make the book authoritative.

Q. Would you be willing to concede that the book is authoritative, while reserving your right to disagree with any section you choose?

A. No.

Q. Is it your position that there is nothing accurate or of value in the entire 795 pages?

A. What I have seen, I disagree with.

Q. Have you spoken to any of the 18 surgeons who wrote the book, to tell them that you disagree with their conclusions?

A. No.

Q. Have you rejected other books when you have testified in the past?

A. Sure.

Q. Were those also approved medical school textbooks like this one?

A. Some of them were.

Q. Since you refuse to accept this book, or any part of it as authoritative, you realize that I will not be able to cross-examine you with it?

A. Yes, I think that's the rule.

Q. Then let's move on to something else…

Speak to your expert.

Discuss the strengths and weaknesses of both sides of the case. Write down your strongest points, especially those that are incontestable. Ask your expert for cross-examination ideas.

VI

Confronting the Expert

Q. Now Doctor, isn't it true that when a person dies in his sleep, he doesn't know about it until the next morning?
A. Did you actually pass the bar exam?

Face the expert without fear.

The expert witness is a challenge, but she should not be feared. Although she may have impressive credentials and expertise, she is just another witness who must answer your questions.

Experts, in fact, are easier to cross-examine than lay witnesses. First, they are not eyewitnesses; they merely provide opinions, often based on disputed facts. Second, their reports and history as witnesses provide valuable information that is generally unavailable from a lay witness. Third, they are paid well for their time in court, so they are less sympathetic. Finally, they often try to be advocates, and they lose credibility by being pompous, inflexible and unreasonable.

Conduct a voir dire.

Before an expert can render an opinion, the lawyer who calls him must establish his qualifications in the field. To do so, he will ask questions about the expert's education, experience, licenses, experience as a witness, and other pertinent information.

After the witness has provided his background on direct, if you suspect that the expert is not qualified to render an opinion, or his area of expertise is not relevant to the case, then tell the judge that you want to voir dire the witness about his qualifications. Voir dire is Old French for "to speak the truth," and the law allows the lawyer to question a witness (or prospective juror) to determine whether that person is qualified for his appointed role in the case.

The practical effect is that voir dire allows you to confront the witness and conduct a small cross before the main portion of the direct. The questions will be limited to the fitness of the witness to testify, but you may be able to preclude the witness, or limit the scope of his testimony.

Review the expert's file in court.

Before you begin your cross, ask to see the expert's file for the case—the judge will let you review it, and the jurors will welcome a short recess after a technical direct examination.

Read all letters, notes, records and writing in the margins. Compare her report to the one that your adversary sent to you. When the expert does not bring her file to court, question her about her failure to do so:

> Q. Dr. Jung, did you deliberately fail to bring your file to court, or did you neglect to bring it?
> A. I must have forgotten it, subconsciously.

Question his facts, and not his opinion.

The adverse expert will not change his opinion, regardless of the evidence, so you must attack the facts upon which it is based. Ask whether new or different facts "might affect" instead of "would change" his opinion. Although his answer will probably be the same, you will sound more reasonable than the expert:

Instead of:

Q. If you learned that the defendant had been drinking rum all night, would that change your opinion about the cause of the accident?
A. Absolutely not.

Try:

Q. If you learned that the defendant had been drinking rum all night, might that affect your opinion about the cause of the accident?
A. I doubt it.

Reveal the source of his facts.

Q. Did you speak to the plaintiff about how the accident happened?
A. No, I did not.
Q. Do you think that might have been helpful?
A. Not really.
Q. Isn't it usually helpful to get as much information as possible before forming an opinion?
A. Yes, but I read the depositions.
Q. But as an expert, you could have asked further, perhaps better questions of her.
A. I suppose so.
Q. Questions beyond those asked at the deposition.
A. I believe I had enough information.
Q. But she could have provided more information to you.
A. Perhaps.
Q. Did you go to the accident scene?
A. No, I looked at photos.
Q. Do you make a practice of forming opinions based on photographs?
A. I had other information as well.
Q. And much of that information you received from the plaintiff's lawyer.
A. Some of it, not much.

Q. He told you his theory of the case?
A. Yes, basically.
Q. Might it have been helpful to go to the accident scene?
A. Probably not.
Q. So you could tell the jury what you saw there.
A. I told you, I had the photographs.
Q. Did you learn that the jury saw the photographs yesterday, before you came to court?
A. I did not know that.
Q. So, you are showing the jury something that they have already seen for themselves, in the photographs.
A. Right, plus my opinion.
Q. Adding your opinion when they can see for themselves?
A. Yes.

Accentuate the negative.

Determine what the expert could have said on the stand, but did not say. She could have caused damage had she established certain facts and delivered further conclusions, but she never did. Think positively—and accentuate the negative.

Cross the expert about her missing credentials, tests and findings. Prepare to accentuate the negative by applying three steps:

1. The witness testified she did or found X.
2. She could have done or found Y.
3. But she didn't.

The three-step technique usually requires more than three questions, but when done correctly, it minimizes the impact of the expert's testimony. Here is a short example of the three-step technique:

Q. Professor, you said on direct that you conducted the Wheat Germ test.
A. Correct.
Q. The Oatmeal test is commonly used in this kind of case.

A. Not always, but it is a test used.
Q. But you never did the Oatmeal test here.
A. No, I did not.

Highlight the limits of her credentials:

Q. Mrs. Wright, the defense retained you about a month ago.
A. Yes.
Q. You told us that you have a Masters degree in mechanical engineering.
A. That's right.
Q. There is a Ph.D. in your field.
A. Yes, there is.
Q. But you don't have the Ph.D.
A. No.
Q. You also told us you wrote an article on oil tanker design.
A. Yes.
Q. You never wrote a book on the subject.
A. No.
Q. Not even a chapter.
A. No.
Q. Never taught a course on the subject.
A. I've given lectures.
Q. Not at any university.
A. That's true.

Attack the investigation or preparation:

Q. You relied on what the plaintiff's lawyer told you.
A. Well, yes.
Q. You never checked those facts to make sure they were true.
A. I did not.
Q. You never read the hospital chart.
A. Just a few pages of it.
Q. To learn what the doctors in the hospital said about the plaintiff's condition.
A. No.

Q. You never spoke to any of the doctors from the hospital.
A. No.

Minimize the injuries and treatment:

Q. There was no surgery here.
A. Right.
Q. No hospital stay.
A. True.
Q. No fractures.
A. Correct.
Q. No crutches used.
A. Right.
Q. No cane used.
A. I admit that.
Q. No back brace.
A. None.

Address the hypothetical question.

On direct, a lawyer may ask an expert a hypothetical question, in which he recites facts that are in evidence, tells the expert to assume that those facts are true, and then asks for an opinion, based on that assumption. The hypothetical question is persuasive because it summarizes the evidence and then adds the expert's opinion. The question is often quite lengthy and sometimes dramatic.

Listen to the question on direct and make sure that the facts presented are supported by the testimony. When the facts are not accurate, stand and object at the end of the question. Your adversary may have to repeat the entire two-page question. Decide whether it is worth hearing again before you object.

On cross, ask the expert whether he discussed the question with your adversary, and whether any suggestions were made to improve the question. Also, substitute your version of the facts for your adversary's, and ask whether the different facts might affect his opinion.

When the witness refuses to concede that the new facts should logically affect his conclusion, try Max D. Steuer's question:

Q. Will you tell me of anything that could or should be incorporated in that question that would (might) cause you to change your answer?
A. I cannot tell you that.

Argue your case with the expert's report.

Q. Doctor, when you examined Mr. Atlas's lower back, you found restriction of motion.
A. Moderate restriction.
Q. That is a restriction.
A. Yes.
Q. More than a mild restriction.
A. True.
Q. Worse than a mild restriction.
A. Agreed.
Q. That is a positive finding.
A. It is.
Q. Positive in medicine means a problem.
A. You could say that.
Q. Well, positive here is something that is not normal.
A. True.
Q. You also concluded that if the history was correct, that there was a causal connection between the accident and the history.
A. Yes.
Q. And you have no reason to doubt that the history is correct.
A. I have no reason to doubt that.
Q. So if the history is correct, then the accident caused the condition we're talking about here.
A. I would have to agree.

Discuss the expert's fee.

Ask the expert how much he is being paid for his time in court. Do not ask: "How much money are you being paid for your testimony?" That is probably an unfair insinuation, and an objection to the question will be sustained. Ideally, an expert is paid for his time, and not for his testimony. When the witness quotes an hourly rate of pay, ask him whether he has already been paid. If he has been paid, then ask to see the check.

Chastise the glib witness.

When the expert grandstands or volunteers information on cross, let her know that you will not tolerate such conduct:

Q. Dr. Howard, did I ask you anything about whether you sometimes treat patients without payment?
A. No, you didn't.
Q. You just volunteered that to the jury.
A. Yes, I suppose I did.
Q. Now getting back to my question, my company paid you for every visit the plaintiff made to your office, true?
A. Yes.

When the expert provides a rambling, obviously non-responsive narrative, do not stop her. Let her complete her speech while you check your watch or gaze out the window. When she has finished, try a variation of the following:

Q. Professor Harley, is there anything else you would like to add to that before we return to the question that I asked?

Or try James J. Skelton's question:

Q. Doctor, please answer my question first, and then later during re-direct, you can say whatever you like.

Rebuke a claim about the latest research.

When the expert claims that he used scholarly literature supported by the latest research to assist him in reaching his conclusion, ask him whether he brought it to court:

Q. Dr. Gloom, did you bring those articles with you?
A. No.
Q. The jurors will not get to see them, now will they.
A. Sorry, no.

Seek agreement about basic principles.

Establish basic scientific and engineering principles, and other commonly known facts, by asking the expert to agree with your statements:

Q. You would agree Professor that water freezes at 32 degrees Fahrenheit.
A. Yes, I would.
Q. You would also agree that ice begins to melt as the temperature rises above that temperature.
A. I would agree to that, too.

Expose bad science and other nonsense.

When the expert's testimony is strange or incomprehensible, it may in fact be nonsense. Be alert for formulas that are confusing and conclusions that are illogical. Create an analogy to expose a far-fetched or ridiculous proposition.

In one case, the plaintiff claimed that while ascending a subway staircase, she tripped on the top step, which had a riser two inches higher than the other steps, and fell onto the mezzanine floor. She also contended that her eyeglasses cut her right cornea, causing blindness in that eye. Her ophthalmologist testified that, in his opinion, as she fell forward, her glasses tilted forward, and the bottom of the right lens lacerated her right eye. Significantly, she did not have any other injuries to her face, and did not have the glasses. The defense theory was that the plaintiff had cut her eye elsewhere, because the plaintiff's version was implausible. The following exchange took place:

Q. Doctor, it's your opinion that as the plaintiff fell, her glasses tilted at the precise angle required to cut her eye?

A. That's right.
Q. The odds of that happening are pretty remote, wouldn't you say?
A. I would agree.
Q. Sort of like tossing a coin and having it land on its edge.
A. Probably not that remote.
Q. Well, in your 35 years of medical practice, how many times have you seen such a mechanism of injury?
A. Maybe once.

In another case, the plaintiff drove his Cadillac into the rear loader of a sanitation truck that was parked next to a subway station in Brooklyn. The workers had parked the truck there in order to empty the trash containers down in the subway. The truck had its emergency flashers on, but the plaintiff's expert testified that the men should have placed orange cones around the truck, in order to provide adequate warning to oncoming motorists. That opinion was questionable, and some fishing was required to determine its source. The expert's answer on cross was pure gold for the questioner:

Q. Sir, you told us on direct that the men should have placed cones around the truck.
A. That's right.
Q. You have seen sanitation trucks working on New York streets.
A. Sure I have.
Q. Where have you seen men using cones during a pick-up.
A. On the FDR Drive [an expressway on the east side of Manhattan].
Q. The FDR Drive! Are you serious?
A. Well, yes.
Q. Are you telling this jury that you have seen garbage trucks stop on the FDR Drive, and men place cones around it so they could empty trash containers?
A. (With much less confidence) Yes?
Q. That's something you don't see every day, is it.
A. No, not really.
Q. And you've never seen it before or since.
A. Not there, no.

Finally, take note when an engineer explains how vector forces, counterweights, Newtonian physics and other mechanisms caused an accident, while he creates a jumbled, Jackson Pollack chart with sketches, arrows and numbers:

Q. Tell us, Mr. Brady, which part of your chart, here, should the jury focus on?
A. No part in particular.
Q. Do you think it will help them decide the case?
A. I have no idea.

Dismiss the kitchen sink testimony.

Experts sometimes add new contentions on the witness stand. They become overconfident and pad the evidence, because they think they can get away with it. Be alert and expose the creative testimony. The approach shown next is an alternative to impeachment:

Q. Sir, the claim here is that the steps were unsafe because they were slippery, true?
A. There were problems with the handrails, the risers, the concrete, the width, the steepness, and everything else, too.
Q. Yes, that's what you just told us, but your only claim here is that the steps were slippery, right?
A. Well, yes, too slippery.
Q. Your report has no claim of defective handrails.
A. True.
Q. Or riser heights.
A. Correct.
Q. Or treads, or steepness, or anything else.
A. I don't understand your point.
Q. Wasn't that long list of problems you just mentioned, something new in this case?
A. I wouldn't say new.
Q. You just added all of those problems now on the cross-examination.
A. Some of them.

Q. And they were never part of this case, at any time before today.
A. Right.

The overconfident expert often believes he is unstoppable. Isadore "Izzy" Halpern shows how to lead him into absurdity:

Q. Doctor, you testified that the plaintiff suffers from aphasia?
A. Yes, she does.
Q. And neuralgia.
A. Yes.
Q. And also paresthesia.
A. Correct.
Q. And of course, Polynesia.
A. Of course.
Q. Isn't Polynesia an island group in the Pacific Ocean?
A. (No answer).

Beware of unusually large numbers.

Some experts, such as economists, provide opinions with astronomical, Treasury Department amounts that are much too high (or less often, much too low). Check their figures, and make sure they conform to reality.

In one case, a plaintiff who suffered catastrophic injuries required the assistance of a home care attendant. His economist concluded that because he would need an attendant sixteen hours a day for life, the cost would be $14,000,000. Several months after the economist prepared his report, the plaintiff's doctor determined that his needs had changed, and that his condition required permanent twenty-four hour care, which, logically, would increase the projected home care cost by fifty percent. At trial, the economist said the following:

Q. Mr. Ross, you told us the home care cost would be $14,000,000?
A. Yes.
Q. Based on a sixteen hour day?
A. That is correct.

Q. But you have since learned that the plaintiff's doctor now recommends twenty-four-hour care.
A. I did learn that.
Q. That would affect the lifetime cost.
A. It would.
Q. It would, in fact, add fifty percent to your figures.
A. That's about right, yes.
Q. Have you adjusted your projected amount to reflect the new need for twenty-four-hour care?
A. No, I am going to stand by the figures in my report.
Q. (Loudly, and with emphasis) So you are telling the jury to forget about the extra seven million dollars that the plaintiff will need for home care!?
Opposing Counsel: Objection!
The Court: Yes, sustained. Counsel, you just did that for the jury.
Q. Your Honor, everything I do here is for the jury.
The Court: Well, stay away from that.

In summation, the point was made that if the economist was willing to ignore seven million dollars, just imagine how inflated the original figures were! (That comment also drew an objection.)

Correct the expert who re-phrases.

Experts often try to avoid a question by creating their own question. Raymond J. Furey calls this technique a jailbreak. The witness tries to break free from your question and answer a question she wishes you had asked. She will begin her answer with: "Are you asking me," or "if you are asking me," and then re-phrase your question. When that happens, reject the question and re-state your question:

Q. Mr. Wilbur, did you conduct a coefficient of friction test?
A. Are you asking me if I thought that a coefficient of friction test would be helpful here?
Q. No, that was not my question. Please listen again. My question was: Did you conduct a coefficient of friction test?
A. Oh. No, I did not.

Or try:

Q. Let me ask my question again so there is no mistake. . .

Respond to a question.

An expert or lay witness will sometimes blurt out a question, often in frustration, such as: "What was I supposed to do, Counselor," or "what would you have done?" Since the lawyer's job is to ask questions, and not to answer them, a reasonable response is a gentle rejoinder that includes what the witness could have done:

A. Look Counselor, what should I have done?
Q. Sir, I am not allowed to answer your questions, but did you: (clear the building; adjust the medication; walk away)?

Keep it simple.

Explain the issues so that the jurors understand your points on cross. With experts, show the jury that you understand the subject matter, while keeping it simple. Use analogies with everyday words, and define difficult terms yourself, until the witness accepts your definition.

Be respectful.

Be polite and show respect, especially to physicians, but be firm when you must. When a witness uses the title Doctor, refer to him as such, even if the title is his own creation, such as The Doctor of Love. Good manners always enhance a good cross.

Tell the jurors you will cross-examine.

During jury selection, inform the jurors about the order of trial, and tell them that you will cross any witness the other side calls. Let them know that you may have to press the witnesses for answers.

When the court rules permit you to voir dire prospective jurors, try a variation of this statement:

> Counsel: My adversary here will call witnesses, and conduct what is called direct examination. After she is done with the direct, I get a chance to take a crack at the witness on what is called cross-examination. Even if you have never been in court before, you have seen it done in movies, on TV, and you've read about it, too. I'm going to cross the witnesses and my questions are probably going to be tougher than Counsel's. I may have to press them for information you didn't hear on direct. Is that okay with you? I see smiles, and you're probably thinking: "That's what we came to see, Counselor." As long as we're clear on that, fine.

When you are not permitted to speak to the prospective jurors, use a similar approach in your opening statement, without the questions or comments.

Have patience and confidence.

Take your time, be patient, lay a foundation and develop a rhythm. Show poise and confidence throughout the examination. Maintain a poker face when stung by an answer, and move on to your next point. Remember too, that with each question and answer, you are talking to the jury.

Some examinations will be difficult, or even worse. Grit your teeth and forge ahead. Remember to get the last word, even if it is:

Q. Has that about covered your presentation, Professor?
A. I think that's about it.
Q. Well, that's all, for now.

VII

Tips for Trial Practice

Slow down and take it easy, Counselor. You'll live longer.

– Judge Joseph J. Dowd

Arrive early.

Go to the courtroom early and meet the court staff. When late, apologize without an excuse. Obtain the telephone numbers of the courtroom and the judge's chambers. Ask whether the judge has any unusual requirements or pet peeves. Be kind to the court personnel and remember: "The judge can hurt you, but the clerk can kill you" (Judge Joseph Levine).

Stand for the judge and jury.

Unless you are told otherwise, stand when the judge or jury enters and leaves the courtroom. In open court, address the judge as Your Honor, but Judge is fine at the bench or in chambers.

Answer the judge's question.

The judge will ask counsel difficult questions. When she asks a question, answer it first, and then explain further, if necessary.

Represent your client zealously.

Learn the facts and the law, and represent your client with vigor and enthusiasm, within the bounds of the law.

Develop and preserve a good reputation.

Earn a reputation as a tough, but fair and honest advocate. Avoid any conduct that could jeopardize your standing in the Bar. With the judge and jury, build credibility slowly, and always be their best guide to the truth.

Keep fit.

Find a program to keep yourself fit, eat sensibly, and get enough sleep.

Learn to relax.

Trying cases is a strenuous business. Learn how to relax, roll with the punches, and be sure to laugh often, especially at yourself.

There is always room at the top.

–Daniel Webster

About the Author

Peter D. Polchinski practices law in New York City. He was a homicide prosecutor for the Manhattan District Attorney's Office and National Trial Counsel for a company in asbestos litigation. He was also trial counsel for the families of the pilots in the Avianca Air Disaster case. He developed and has taught six Continuing Legal Education courses, was Chief Instructor for the Hofstra Law School Summer Trial Course, and teaches in the Manhattan District Attorney's Trial Advocacy Program. A graduate of Suffolk County Community College and Stony Brook University, he received his J.D. from Fordham University School of Law and an LL.M. in Trade Regulation from New York University School of Law.

Index

S-U

V-Z

The Winning Edge: Effective Communication and Persuasion Techniques for Lawyers

by Richard H. Lucas, Ph.D. and K. Byron McCoy, J.D.

With this easy-to-read book, you will discover the hidden keys that turn a good lawyer into a great lawyer. If you want to improve your effectiveness in the courtroom, establish genuine rapport with a jury, and achieve maximum results in litigation, then you will want *The Winning Edge* for your reference library.

You will learn about the four essential elements of successful communication, the keys to establishing rapport, the importance of metaprograms, and enhancing your performance--into the winning performance. You can implement these successful strategies immediately. You may be assured that accomplished lawyers utilize this knowledge where and when it counts--during opening and closing arguments, witness and client interviews, jury selection and observation, and direct and cross examinations. Utilize this book to learn these advanced and proven techniques in the courtroom. With *The Winning Edge*, you will know why and how these techniques work and achieve maximum results for your clients in the courtroom time and time again.

Product Code: 5384 • ISBN: 978-0-913875-38-4
Pages: 220 • Softbound • Size: 6x9

The Persuasive Edge

by Richard J. Crawford, Ph.D. and Charlotte A. Morris, M.A.

The Persuasive Edge is a must for every trial lawyer, teacher and student of law or communication, and anyone else whose practice or profession depends on human persuasion.

This straight-forward discussion combines the best academic conclusions from the psychology of human persuasion and decision-making with the practical knowledge acquired from litigation throughout the United States, to offer you a more purposeful and practical approach to improving your influence and advocacy. The authors' extensive experience as trial consultants has given them the opportunity to test modern persuasion techniques and research by working inside jury trials and conducting interviews with thousands of real and mock jurors in a wide variety of civil and criminal cases and training opportunities. This wealth of experience and unique perspective will assist you in creating a persuasive strategy for all aspects of legal practice but especially within the jury trial. This book is not an abstract discussion of communication and persuasion theory, but a reference work designed to offer you practical and concrete techniques for improving your persuasive communication skills.

This new edition offers updated and practical suggestions for the effective use of advanced technology to visually enhance your persuasive strategy for every jury trial, and provides rare and insightful advice about improving your persuasive effectiveness and influence with judges.

Regardless of your specialty or years of experience, your advocacy will be enhanced by the deliberate communication choices identified and illustrated in this book. For everyone working, teaching or studying in the legal arena, this advanced guide to purposeful persuasion will change the way you communicate for the better.

Product Code: 6737 • ISBN: 978-1-930056-73-2
Pages: 304 • Casebound • Size: 6x9